Alphabet Alliteration

Bilingual French-English

Copyright 2012 © Adele Marie Crouch

All rights reserved. No part of this publication

may be reproduced or transmitted in any form or by

any means, electronic or mechanical, including photocopy,

recording, or any information storage and retrieval system,

without permission in writing from the author.

Requests for permission to make copies of any part of the work should be submitted online to Adele@creationsbycrouch.com or mailed to Adele Marie Crouch, P.O. Box 322, Elfrida, AZ 85610

www.creationsbycrouch.com

Acknowledgements

Without the continued support of my wonderful husband and best friend, Doug, this work would not have come to fruition. His hours of dedication and assistance to my projects keep me on track. For that I am eternally grateful.

To every teacher, parent, sister, brother, aunt, uncle and grandparent who reads to children I thank you.

Aunt Abby ate an apple

Tante Abby a mangé une pomme

**apple
pomme**

Busy bees buzzed on the blooms

Les abeilles actives ont bourdonné dans les fleurs

bee
abeilles

Chris caught Cathy's cat

Chris a attrapé le chat de Cathy

cat
chat

Dave's dancing dog delighted Daisy

Le chien dansant de Dave a ravi Cathy

**dog
chien**

Ed's elephant eats eggplant

L'éléphant de Ed mange une aubergine

elephant

éléphant

Fred found four frogs on Friday

Fred a trouvé quatre grenouilles ce Vendredi

frog

grenouille

Gary grew green grapes

Gary a fait pousser des raisins verts

grapes

raisins

Henry the Hippopotamus is happy

L'hippopotame d'Henry est content

Hippopotamus
Hippopotame

Ivan itches in an icy igloo

Ca démange Ivan dans l'igloo glacé

igloo

igloo

Jill's jack-rabbit jumped over Jim's jelly jar

Le lièvre de Jill a sauté par-dessus le pot de confiture de Jim

jack-rabbit
lièvre

King Kirby kept Kenneth's kickball

Le roi Kirby a gardé le ballon de Kenneth

king
roi

Larry lost Lucy's lucky locket

Larry a perdu le médaillon porte-bonheur de Lucy

locket

médaillon

Mike's mouse moved to the music

La souris de Mike a bougé en musique

mouse
souris

Nancy's neighbor nets a newt

Le voisin de Nancy a pêché un triton

newt
triton

Ollie the octopus is out in the ocean

Ollie la pieuvre est de sortie dans l'océan

octopus

pieuvre

Puff the porcupine played in a puddle

Puff le porc-épic a joué dans une flaque

porcupine

porc-épic

Quinton quilted quality quilts

Quinton a brodé des couettes de qualité

quilt

couettes

Robert's red rooster ran in the race

Le coq rouge de Robert a couru dans la course

rooster

coq

Suzy's spaceship sailed to the stars

La fusée de Suzy a volé vers les étoiles

spaceship

fusée

Tom trapped ten tadpoles on Tuesday

Tom a piégé dix têtards ce mardi

tadpole
têtard

Uncle Uggy's umbrella unfolded

Le parapluie d'oncle Uggy s'est ouvert

umbrella
parapluie

Veronica viewed the violet vase

Véronica a observé le vase violet

vase colored violet

vase de couleur violette

William watched Waldo the walrus wiggle

William a regardé Waldo le morse rigoler

walrus

morse

Xylene x-rayed Xanna's Xerus

Xylène a passé aux rayons X le xérus de Xanna

xerus (African squirrel)
xérus (écureuil africain)

Yolanda's yellow yak yawned yesterday

Le yak jaune de Yolande a baillé hier

yak
yak

Ziva zipped up her zipper

Ziva a remonté sa fermeture éclair

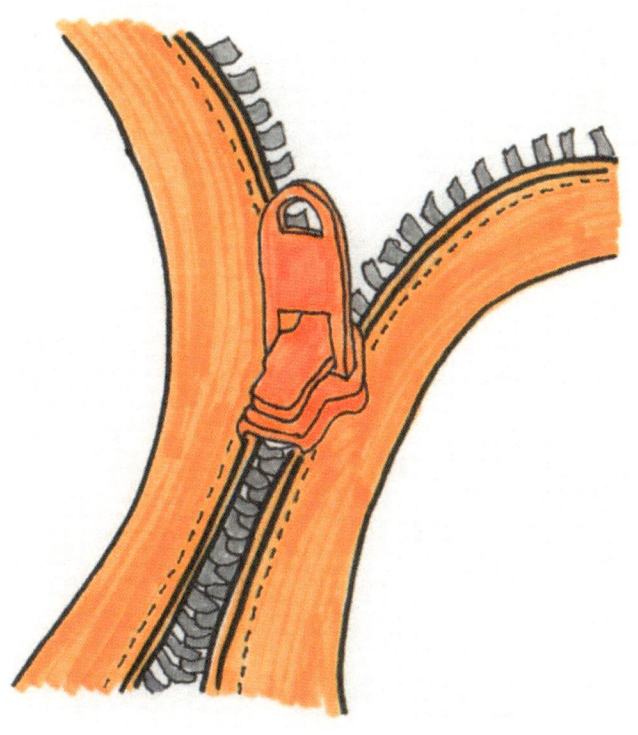

zipper
fermeture éclair

About the Author

"Alphabet Alliteration" is a new twist on an old subject, learning the English alphabet. "How The Fox Got His Color" and "Where Hummingbirds Come From" are picture books for children ages 3 - 6 years of age. "The Dance of The Caterpillars", a lesson in prepositions is designed for 2nd grade students. "The Gnomes of Knot-Hole Manor" is a chapter book targeting 3rd graders. It teaches words with silent letters and words that sound the same but are spelled differently.

"Catherine's Travels" is an historic novel that takes place in Missouri during the 1800's. Catherine and her family flee war torn Austria seeking a new life in America. Disaster strikes and Catherine finds herself alone in the wilderness.

"Catherine's Travels Book 2 ~ Lawson's Search" After Lawson's beautiful wife, Catherine, is kidnapped he embarks on a search that will take him across the United States, over the Rocky Mountains and into the land of the Navajo. Catherine will take a terrifying, yet rewarding journey with her husband's starch enemy. Blue Eyes goes on a vision quest that will change his life forever.

Adele is an artist as well as a published author. Her books are currently available on the internet (Amazon), through her web site (http://www.creationsbycrouch.com), and on Kindle.

Adele's children's books have become popular with English as a second language students and foreign language students all over the world and are on the top 10 list of ESL study material on Amazon. Her website is filled with study material to help people study foreign languages. It includes - vocabulary lists, MP3 files, and even has a list of the questions you need to know to pass the US citizenship exam. All of this is free to the viewer. See: www.creationsbycrouch.com

If you wish to contact Adele, you can email: Adele@creationsbycrouch.com

Printed in Great Britain
by Amazon.co.uk, Ltd.,
Marston Gate.